# The Best
# Husband
# in the World!

THIS IS A PRION BOOK

First published in Great Britain in 2016 by Prion
An imprint of the Carlton Publishing Group
20 Mortimer Street
London W1T 3JW

Copyright 2016 © Carlton Publishing Group

A CIP catalogue for this book is available from the British Library.

ISBN 978-1-85375-953-6

Printed in Dubai

10 9 8 7 6 5 4 3 2 1

The Best
# Husband
in the World!

Humorous and Inspirational Quotes
Celebrating the Perfect Partner

**PRION**

# Contents

# Introduction

In the 21st century, being a husband is a lot like having a job: nobody really wants to be there, the boss is a micro-managing tyrant and you're forever wondering where all your wages go. But, don't worry, it doesn't last long. Before you know it you'll be made redundant and replaced, rather bizarrely, by your own children. Such is life.

Thankfully, *The Best Husband in the World!* is here to cheer you up. Sadly, it doesn't contain pop-up lap dances, free cold beer tokens or a hall pass to a week off marriage. But it does include 350 of the wittiest husband-related quotes ever – enough merriment and wisdom to help you remember that married life is meant to be enjoyed, not simply endured. Off you go… Enjoy!

# Boys Will Be Boys

"Boys will be boys and so will a lot of middle-aged men."

*Kin Hubbard*

"The first thing men notice about a woman is her eyes. Then, when her eyes aren't looking, they notice her breasts."

*Conan O'Brien*

"In 1969 I gave up women and
alcohol, and it was the worst
20 minutes of my life."

*George Best*


"You don't appreciate a lot of stuff
in school until you get older. Little
things like being spanked every day
by a middle-aged woman: stuff you
pay good money for in later life."

*Emo Philips*

"God gave us all a penis and a brain, but only enough blood to run one at a time."

*Robin Williams*

"Some people think having large breasts makes a woman stupid. Actually, it's quite the opposite: a woman having large breasts makes men stupid."

*Rita Rudner*

"Life expectancy would grow
by leaps and bounds if green
vegetables smelled as good
as bacon."

*Doug Larson*

"If you spend any time with a
man, you'll realize that we're
all still little boys."

*Paul Walker*

"Whenever I feel the need
to exercise, I lie down until
it goes away."

*Paul Terry*


"I have a lot of growing up to do.
I realized that the other day
inside my fort."

*Zach Galifianakis*

"Alcohol is a misunderstood
vitamin."

*P.G. Wodehouse*

"Bachelors should be heavily taxed.
It is not fair that some men should
be happier than others."

*Oscar Wilde*

"Nothing is forever, if you have
enough power tools."

*S.A. Sachs*

"Put your hand on a hot stove for
a minute and it seems like an hour.
Sit with a pretty girl for an hour
and it seems like a minute.
That's relativity."

*Albert Einstein*

"It is assured that men of all ages imagine a woman naked when they first meet."

*Tiffany Madison*

"One frequently only finds out how really beautiful a woman is, until after considerable acquaintance with her."

*Mark Twain*

"There is a correlation between the number of days since a man last had sex and the number of things that he is willing to do for a woman."

*Mokokoma Mokhonoana*

"Getting married for sex is like buying a 747 for the free peanuts."

*Jeff Foxworthy*

"No married man is genuinely
happy if he has to drink worse
whisky than he used to drink
when he was single."

*H.L. Mencken*

"A man is never completely alone
in this world. At the worst, he has
the company of a boy, a youth,
and by and by a grown man –
the one he used to be."

*Cesare Pavese*

"When a woman is talking to you, listen to what she says with her eyes."

*Victor Hugo*

"I like threesomes with two women, not because I'm a cynical sexual predator. Oh no! But because I'm a romantic. I'm looking for The One. And I'll find her more quickly if I audition two at a time."

*Russell Brand*

"I am always looking for meaningful one night stands."

*Dudley Moore*

"I feel sorry for people who don't drink. When they wake up in the morning, that's as good as they're going to feel all day."

*Frank Sinatra*

"When it comes to hiding porn,
every man is a CIA agent."

*S.A. Sachs*

"All women should know how to
take care of children. Most of them
will have a husband some day."

*Franklin P. Jones*

"If you can make a woman laugh,
you can make her do anything."

*Marilyn Monroe*


"Trust me, Bart, it's better to walk
in on both your parents than on
just one of them."

*Homer Simpson*

"Nothing is really work unless
you would rather be doing
something else."

*J.M. Barrie*

"Progress isn't made by early risers.
It's made by lazy men trying to find
easier ways to do something."

*Robert A. Heinlein*

"Some people are boys longer
than others."

*Patricia Briggs*

"The main reason Santa is so jolly
is because he knows where all the
bad girls live."

*George Carlin*

# Modern
# Family

"It is quality rather than quantity
that matters."

*Seneca*

"Here's all you have to know
about men and women: women are
crazy, men are stupid. And the main
reason women are crazy is that
men are stupid."

*George Carlin*

"Smile at each other, make time for
each other in your family."

*Mother Teresa*

"A happy home is one in which
each spouse grants the possibility
that the other may be right, though
neither believes it."

*Don Fraser*

"My wife is a sex object. Every time I ask for sex, she objects."

*Les Dawson*


"Kids. They're not easy. But there has to be some penalty for sex."

*Bill Maher*

"One of the symptoms of an approaching nervous breakdown is the belief that one's work is terribly important."

*Bertrand Russell*

"I've heard that hard work never killed anyone, but I say why take the chance?"

*Ronald Reagan*

"I'm not saying my wife's a bad
cook, but she uses a smoke
alarm as a timer."

*Bob Monkhouse*

"Whenever I read the newspaper,
I say to myself, 'At least my
wife loves me.'"

*Bill Gross*

"For a man wins nothing better than
a good wife, and then again nothing
deadlier than a bad one."

*Hesiod*

"I'd rather lose an argument
than get into a long discussion
in order to win it."

*Rafael Nadal*

"If you want your wife to listen to you, then talk to another woman; she will be all ears."

*Sigmund Freud*

"My wife dresses to kill. She cooks the same way."

*Henry Youngman*

"It's not easy to juggle a pregnant wife and a troubled child, but somehow I managed to fit in eight hours of TV a day."

*Homer Simpson*

"If women are expected to do the same work as men, we must teach them the same things."

*Plato*

"A man is basically as faithful
as his options."

*Chris Rock*

"Why bother with Google when
I have a wife who knows everything
about everything!"

*Akshay Kumar*

"Being a husband is a whole-time job. That is why so many husbands fail. They cannot give their entire attention to it."

*Arnold Bennett*

"It is not flesh and blood but the heart which makes us fathers and sons."

*Johann Schiller*

"Before I got married I had six
theories about bringing up children;
now I have six children and
no theories."

*John Wilmot*

"Before I met my husband,
I'd never fallen in love. I'd stepped
in it a few times."

*Rita Rudner*

"I don't sit around thinking that
I'd like to have another husband;
only another man would make me
think that way."

*Lauren Bacall*

"I am about to be married and am
of course in all the misery of a man
in pursuit of happiness."

*Lord Byron*

"What I say is that, if a man really likes potatoes, he must be a pretty decent sort of fellow."

*A.A. Milne*

"A mother takes 20 years to make a man of her boy, and another woman makes a fool of him in 20 minutes."

*Robert Frost*

"I think every girl's dream is to find a bad boy at the right time, when he wants to not be bad anymore."

*Taylor Swift*

"A retired husband is often a wife's full-time job."

*Ella Harris*

"Marriage is indeed a
manoeuvring business."

*Jane Austen*

"A lot of good arguments are
spoiled by some fool who knows
what he is talking about."

*Miguel de Unamuno*

"Arguments are to be avoided:
they are always vulgar and
often convincing."

*Oscar Wilde*


"'Tis strange what a man may
do and a woman yet think
him an angel."

*William Makepeace Thackeray*

"Marrying a man is like buying something you've been admiring for a long time in a shop window. You may love it when you get it home, but it doesn't always go with everything else in the house."

*Jean Kerr*

"There is no spectacle on earth more appealing than that of a beautiful woman in the act of cooking dinner for someone she loves."

*Thomas Wolfe*

"O my love, my wife!
Death, that hath suck'd the
honey of thy breath
Hath had no power yet upon
thy beauty."

*William Shakespeare*

"Before you marry a person, you
should first make them use a
computer with slow Internet service
to see who they really are."

*Will Ferrell*

"I thought I was promiscuous, but it turns out I was just thorough."

*Russell Brand*

"Men want a woman whom they can turn on and off like a light switch."

*Ian Fleming*

"Better to remain silent and be thought a fool than to speak out and remove all doubt."

*Abraham Lincoln*

"Too often the strong, silent man is silent only because he does not know what to say, and is reputed strong only because he has remained silent."

*Winston Churchill*

"The world would be happier if men had the same capacity to be silent that they have to speak."

*Baruch Spinoza*

"Marriage is three parts love and seven parts forgiveness of sins."

*Lao Tzu*

"Setting a good example for children takes all the fun out of middle age."

*William Feather*

"The supreme art of war is to subdue the enemy without fighting."

*Sun Tzu*

"The man as he converses is the lover; silent, he is the husband."

*Honore de Balzac*

"All that a husband or wife really wants is to be pitied a little, praised a little, and appreciated a little."

*Oliver Goldsmith*

"To love someone deeply gives you strength. Being loved by someone deeply gives you courage."

*Lao Tzu*


"Children are smarter than any of us. Know how I know that? I don't know one child with a full-time job and children."

*Bill Hicks*

"Whenever I fail as a father or husband... a toy and a diamond always works."

*Shah Rukh Khan*

"To catch a husband is an art; to hold him is a job."

*Simone de Beauvoir*

"I've never yet met a man who could look after me. I don't need a husband. What I need is a wife."

*Joan Collins*

"A friend never defends a husband who gets his wife an electric skillet for her birthday."

*Erma Bombeck*

"The most important thing a father can do for his children is to love their mother."

*Theodore Hesburg*

"An archaeologist is the best husband a woman can have. The older she gets the more interested he is in her."

*Agatha Christie*

"Guys do not get enough credit for being domestic. This is because the people who give out the credits for being domestic are – not to generalize or anything – women."

*Dave Barry*

"Where thou art, that is home."

*Emily Dickinson*

"I hate when new parents ask who the baby looks like. It was born 15 minutes ago, it looks like a potato."

*Will Ferrell*


"My Dad is a proper family man. He's got three of them."

*Steve Bugeja*

"By working faithfully eight hours
a day you may eventually get to be
boss and work 12 hours a day."

*Robert Frost*

"A husband is what is left of a lover,
after the nerve has been extracted."

*Helen Rowland*

"Those people who think they know everything are a great annoyance to those of us who do."

*Isaac Asimov*

"Men have higher body temperatures than women. If your heating goes out in winter, I recommend sleeping next to a man. Men are like portable heaters that snore."

*Rita Rudner*

"Middle age is when you're sitting at home on a Saturday night and the telephone rings and you hope it isn't for you."

*Ogden Nash*

"In a perfect world, no man, including the husband, would ever be invited to a baby shower."

*Jason Love*

"Insanity is hereditary.
You get it from your children."

*Sam Levenson*


"Youth is when you're allowed
to stay up late on New Year's Eve.
Middle age is when you're
forced to."

*Bill Vaughn*

"The greatest deception men suffer
is from their own opinions."

*Leonardo da Vinci*

"In life we shall find many men that
are great, and some that are good,
but very few men that are both
great and good."

*Charles Caleb Colton*

"One half of the world cannot
understand the pleasures
of the other."

*Jane Austen*

"The true index of a man's
character is the health of his wife."

*Cyril Connolly*

# The Missus

"A woman drove me to drink
and I never even had the
courtesy to thank her."

*W.C. Fields*

"All a girl really wants from a guy
is for him to prove to her that they
are not all the same."

*Marilyn Monroe*

"You – poor and obscure, and small and plain as you are – I entreat to accept me as a husband."

*Mr Rochester, Jane Eyre, Charlotte Brontë*

"Plain women are always jealous of their husbands. Beautiful women never are. They are always so occupied with being jealous of other women's husbands."

*Oscar Wilde*

"Single women have a dreadful propensity for being poor. Which is one very strong argument in favour of matrimony."

*Jane Austen*

"For women, the best aphrodisiacs are words. The G-spot is in the ears. He who looks for it below there is wasting his time."

*Isabel Allende*

"Women look in a mirror, and no matter what they look like in real life, they alway think they look worse. Guys look in a mirror and think they look substantially better than they are. No matter how much of a three-toed knuckle dragger a guy is, he figures he's four or five sit-ups away from being in the hot tub with Elle McPherson."

*Richard Jeni*

"No woman gets an orgasm from shining the kitchen floor."

*Betty Friedan*

"Of all the home remedies, a good wife is best."

*Kin Hubbard*

"Choose a wife rather by your ear than your eye."

*Thomas Fuller*

"I admit that my wife is outspoken,
but by whom?"

*Sam Levenson*


"At the age of 11 or thereabouts
women acquire a poise and an
ability to handle difficult situations
which a man, if he is lucky,
manages to achieve somewhere
in the late seventies."

*P.G. Wodehouse*

"Male menopause is a lot more
fun than female menopause.
With female menopause you gain
weight and get hot flashes. Male
menopause – you get to date young
girls and drive motorcycles."

*Rita Rudner*

"My wife doesn't care what I do
when I'm away, as long as I don't
have a good time."

*Lee Trevino*

"I wouldn't be caught dead marrying a woman old enough to be my wife."

*Tony Curtis*

"There's a reason it's called 'girls gone wild' and not 'women gone wild'. When girls go wild, they show their tits. When women go wild, they kill men and drown their kids in a tub."

*Louis CK*

"The woman who can't influence
her husband to vote the way
she wants ought to be
ashamed of herself."

*E.M. Forster*

"My wife heard me say I love you a
thousand times, but she never once
heard me say sorry."

*Bruce Willis*

"I love my wife dearly, and,
therefore, I've never cooked a meal,
romantic or otherwise, for her."

*Steve Carell*


"Husband: a man with hopes
of being a lover who settles for
being a provider, causing his wife
to grow suspicious of her depleting
jewellery box."

*Bauvard*

"Women speak because they wish to speak, whereas a man speaks only when driven to speech by something outside himself – like, for instance, he can't find any clean socks."

*Jean Kerr*

"Man does not control his own fate. The women in his life do that for him."

*Groucho Marx*

"I like 'em big. And stupid. Don't tell my husband."

*Meg Cabot*

"You can't stay married in a situation where you are afraid to go to sleep in case your wife might cut your throat."

*Mike Tyson*

"Bigamy is having one wife too many. Monogamy is the same."

*Oscar Wilde*

"Take my wife... Please!"

*Henny Youngman*

"My wife was too beautiful for words, but not for arguments."

*John Barrymore*

"I give unto my wife my second best
bed with the furniture."

*William Shakespeare*

"There's very little advice in men's
magazines, because men don't
think there's a lot they don't know.
Women do. Women want to learn.
Men think, 'I know what I'm doing,
just show me somebody naked.'"

*Jerry Seinfeld*

"The wife's run off with the bloke
next door. I do miss him."

*Les Dawson*

"Men are superior to women.
For one thing, men can urinate
from a speeding car."

*Will Durst*

"A good husband makes
a good wife."

*John Florio*

"Feminism is not a fad. It's not like Angry Birds. Although it does involve a lot of angry birds. Bad example."

*Bridget Christie*

"A dress that zips up the back will bring a husband and wife together."

*James H. Boren*

"The secret of a happy marriage
remains a secret."

*Henry Youngman*

"I know a man who gave up
smoking, drinking, sex and rich
food. He was healthy right up to
the time he killed himself."

*Johnny Carson*

"The only time a woman really succeeds in changing a man is when he's a baby."

*Natalie Wood*


"Marriage is a wonderful institution, but who wants to live in an institution?"

*Groucho Marx*

"Housework is what a woman does
that nobody notices unless she
hasn't done it."

*Evan Esar*


"If a girl looks swell when
she meets you, who gives a
damn if she's late?"

*J.D. Salinger*

"Middle age is the time when a man
is always thinking that in a week or
two he will feel as good as ever."

*Don Marquis*

"A man is already halfway in
love with any woman who
listens to him."

*Brendan Francis*

"The most precious possession that ever comes to a man in this world is a woman's heart."

*Josiah G. Holland*

"It is easier to be a lover than a husband for the simple reason that it is more difficult to be witty every day than to say pretty things from time to time."

*Honore de Balzac*

"Let the wife make the husband glad to come home, and let him make her sorry to see him leave."

*Martin Luther*


"An ideal wife is any woman who has an ideal husband."

*Booth Tarkington*

"It's not beauty but fine qualities,
my girl, that keep a husband."

*Euripides*

"Real love amounts to withholding
the truth, even when you're offered
the perfect opportunity to hurt
someone's feelings."

*David Sedaris*

"Women are meant to be loved,
not to be understood."

*Oscar Wilde*

"A diplomat is a man who always
remembers a woman's birthday, but
never remembers her age."

*Robert Frost*

# Until Death
# Do Us Part

"I got gaps; you got gaps; we fill each other's gaps."

*Rocky Balboa*

"The longest sentence you can form with two words is: I do."

*H.L. Mencken*

"My husband and I have never considered divorce... murder sometimes, but never divorce."

*Joyce Brothers*

"Marriage is like a coffin and each kid is another nail."

*Homer Simpson*

"Love seems the swiftest but it is the slowest of all growths. No man or woman really knows what perfect love is until they have been married a quarter of a century."

*Mark Twain*

"A good marriage would be between
a blind wife and a deaf husband."

*Michel de Montaigne*

"Paying alimony is like feeding
hay to a dead horse."

*Groucho Marx*

"The course of true love never
did run smooth."

*William Shakespeare*

"Those who divorce aren't necessarily the most unhappy, just those neatly able to believe their misery is caused by one other person."

*Alain de Botton*

"In every marriage more than a week old, there are grounds for divorce. The trick is to find and continue to find grounds for marriage."

*Robert Anderson*

"I support gay marriage. I believe gay people have a right to be as miserable as the rest of us."

*Kinky Friedman*

"The husband who decides to surprise his wife is often very much surprised himself."

*Voltaire*

"Love many things, for therein lies the true strength, and whosoever loves much performs much, and can accomplish much, and what is done in love is done well."

*Vincent van Gogh*

"I first learned the concept of non-violence in my marriage."

*Gandhi*

"Many marriages would be better if the husband and the wife clearly understood that they are on the same side."

*Zig Ziglar*

"I was married by a judge. I should have asked for a jury."

*Groucho Marx*

"The best way to remember your
wife's birthday is to forget it once."

*E. Joseph Cossman*


"Instead of getting married again,
I'm going to find a woman I don't
like and just give her a house."

*Rod Stewart*

"It is easier to build strong children
than to repair broken men."

*Frederick Douglass*


"Love is a lot like a backache.
It doesn't show up on X-rays,
but you know it's there."

*George Burns*


"Never trust a husband too far,
nor a bachelor too near."

*Helen Rowland*

"Love is the answer, but while you're waiting for the answer, sex raises some pretty good questions."

*Woody Allen*

"Marriage is really tough because you have to deal with feelings and lawyers."

*Richard Pryor*

"And she's got brains enough for two, which is the exact quantity the girl who marries you will need."

*P.G. Wodehouse, Mostly Sally*

"By all means, marry. If you get a good wife, you'll become happy; if you get a bad one, you'll become a philosopher."

*Socrates*

"The secrets of success are a
good wife and a steady job.
My wife told me."

*Howard Nemerov*


"All you need for happiness
is a good gun, a good horse
and a good wife."

*Daniel Boone*

"If you would have a good wife,
marry one who has been a
good daughter."

*Thomas Fuller*

"Strike an average between what
a woman thinks of her husband
a month before she marries him
and what she thinks of him a year
afterward, and you will have the
truth about him."

*H.L. Mencken*

"Coming together is a beginning;
keeping together is progress;
working together is success."

*Henry Ford*

"A great marriage is not when the
'perfect couple' comes together.
It is when an imperfect couple
learns to enjoy their differences."

*Dave Meurer*

"There is nothing nobler or more admirable than when two people who see eye to eye keep house as man and wife, confounding their enemies and delighting their friends."

*Homer*

"A lover always thinks of his mistress first and himself second; with a husband it runs the other way."

*Honore de Balzac*

"Chains do not hold a marriage together. It is threads, hundreds of tiny threads, which sew people together through the years."

*Simone Signoret*

"It is a truth universally acknowledged, that a single man in possession of a good fortune, must be in want of a wife."

*Jane Austen*

"A happy marriage is the union
of two good forgivers."

*Robert Quillen*

"Marriage is our last, best
chance to grow up."

*Joseph Barth*

"My wife and I were happy for
20 years. Then we met."

*Rodney Dangerfield*

"Ultimately the bond of all
companionship, whether in
marriage or in friendship,
is conversation."

*Oscar Wilde*


"The great secret of successful
marriage is to treat all disasters
as incidents and none of the
incidents as disasters."

*Harold George Nicolson*

"I don't worry about terrorism.
I was married for two years."
*Sam Kinison*


"Love: the irresistible desire to be
irresistibly desired."
*Mark Twain*


"The goal in marriage is not to
think alike, but to think together."
*Robert C. Dodds*

"A husband without faults is a
dangerous observer."

*George Savile*

"There is no more lovely, friendly
and charming relationship,
communion or company than a
good marriage."

*Martin Luther*

"A smile abroad is often a
scowl at home."

*Alfred, Lord Tennyson*

"More marriages might survive if
the partners realized that sometimes
the better comes after the worse."

*Doug Larson*

"Home is the place we love best
and grumble the most."

*Billy Sunday*

"Marriage is an adventure,
like going to war."

*G.K. Chesterton*

"It's a funny thing that when a man hasn't anything on earth to worry about, he goes off and gets married."

*Robert Frost*

"Keep your eyes wide open before marriage, and half shut afterwards."

*Benjamin Franklin*

"One advantage of marriage is that, when you fall out of love with him or he falls out of love with you, it keeps you together until you fall back in love again."

*Judith Viorst*

"A long marriage is two people trying to dance a duet and two solos at the same time."

*Anne Taylor Fleming*

"Never get married in college;
it's hard to get a start if a
prospective employer finds you've
already made one mistake."

*Elbert Hubbard*

"Only married people understand
you can be miserable and happy
at the same time."

*Chris Rock*

"When my wife and I argue, we're like a band in concert: we start with some new stuff and then we roll out our greatest hits."

*Frank Skinner*

"My wife told me: 'Sex is better on holiday.' That wasn't a very nice postcard to receive."

*Joe Bor*

"My husband wanted to be cremated. I told him I'd scatter his ashes at Neiman Marcus – that way, I'd visit him every day."

*Joan Rivers*

"You come to love not by finding the perfect person, but by seeing an imperfect person perfectly."

*Sam Keen*

"Love at first sight is easy to
understand; it's when two people
have been looking at each other
for a lifetime that it becomes
a miracle."

Sam Levenson


"I snore at night, so I bought a
bunch of those Breathe Right Strips
for my wife to shove in her ears."

Guy Endore-Kaiser

"Seems to me the basic conflict between men and women, sexually, is that men are like firemen. To men, sex is an emergency and no matter what we're doing we can be ready in two minutes. Women, on the other hand, are like fire. They're very exciting, but the conditions have to be exactly right for it to occur."

*Jerry Seinfeld*

"A man will go to war, fight and die for his country. But he won't get a bikini wax."

*Rita Rudner*

"Happy marriages begin when we marry the ones we love, and they blossom when we love the ones we marry."

*Tom Mullen*

"A man's home is his wife's castle."
*Alexander Chase*

"A mother gives you a life, a
mother-in-law gives you her life."
*Amit Kalantri*

"Love is the greatest
refreshment in life."
*Pablo Picasso*

"People say that money is not the key to happiness, but I always figured if you have enough money, you can have a key made."

*Joan Rivers*

"It is a curious thought, but it is only when you see people looking ridiculous that you realize just how much you love them."

*Agatha Christie*

"If I had a flower for every time
I thought of you, I could walk in
my garden forever."

*Alfred, Lord Tennyson*

"Marriage is not kickboxing,
it's salsa dancing."

*Amit Kalantri*

"Love – a temporary insanity
curable by marriage."

*Ambrose Bierce*

"The husband who wants a happy marriage should learn to keep his mouth shut and his checkbook open."

*Groucho Marx*

"There's a way of transferring funds that is even faster than electronic banking. It's called marriage."

*James Holt McGavran*

"Nowadays it's hip not to be married. I'm not interested in being hip."

*John Lennon*

"Marriage is a wonderful invention: then again, so is a bicycle repair kit."

*Billy Connolly*

"I think men who have a pierced ear are better prepared for marriage. They've experienced pain and bought jewellery."

*Rita Rudner*

"Some people claim that marriage interferes with romance. There's no doubt about it. Anytime you have a romance, your wife is bound to interfere."

*Groucho Marx*

"To keep your marriage brimming,
With love in the wedding cup,
Whenever you're wrong, admit it;
Whenever you're right, shut up."

*Ogden Nash*


"Like good wine, marriage gets
better with age – once you learn to
keep a cork in it."

*Gene Perret*

# Man of the
# House

"Men are from Earth, women are from Earth. Deal with it."

*George Carlin*

"Men are reluctant to share our feelings, in large part because we often don't have any."

*Dave Barry*

"Two things only a man cannot hide: that he is drunk and that he is in love."

*Antiphanes*

"Men are only as good as their technical development allows them to be."

*George Orwell*

"Men do not fail;
they give up trying."
*Elihu Root*

"Every man over 40 is a scoundrel."
*George Bernard Shaw*

"By the time a man realizes that his father was right, he has a son who thinks he's wrong."

*Charles Wadsworth*


"What are the three words guaranteed to humiliate men everywhere? 'Hold my purse.'"

*Francois Morency*

"Women want mediocre men,
and men are working to be as
mediocre as possible."

Margaret Mead


"I had a wonderful childhood,
which is tough because it's hard to
adjust to a miserable adulthood."

Larry David

"The male is a domestic animal which, if treated with firmness, can be trained to do most things."

*Jilly Cooper*

"What women want: to be loved, to be listened to, to be desired, to be respected, to be needed, to be trusted, and sometimes, just to be held. What men want: tickets for the world series."

*Dave Barry*

"Beer – the cause and solution to all of life's problems."

*Homer Simpson*

"An easy-going husband is the one indispensable comfort of life."

*Ouida*

"My favourite machine at the gym is the vending machine."

*Caroline Rhea*

"Men want the same thing from their underwear that they want from women: a little bit of support and a little bit of freedom."

*Jerry Seinfeld*

"Women marry men hoping they will change. Men marry women hoping they will not."

*Albert Einstein*

"I love being married. It's so great to find that one special person you want to annoy for the rest of your life."

*Rita Rudner*

"My husband has quite simply been my strength and stay all these years, and I owe him a debt greater than he would ever claim."

*Queen Elizabeth II*

"If a man watches three football games in a row, he should be declared legally dead."

*Erma Bombeck*

"My husband and I didn't sign a prenuptial agreement. We signed a mutual suicide pact."

*Roseanne Barr*

"I promise to be an excellent husband, but give me a wife who, like the moon, will not appear every day in my sky."

*Anton Chekhov*

"A man wants too many things before marriage, but only peace after it."

*Pawan Mishra*

"A man should be taller, older, heavier, uglier, and hoarser than his wife."

*E.W. Howe*

"A good husband is never the first
to go to sleep at night or the last to
awake in the morning."

*Honore de Balzac*

"Don't trust a brilliant idea unless
it survives the hangover."

*Jimmy Breslin*

"The ideal man doesn't exist.
A husband is easier to find."

*Britt Ekland*

"Waste no more time arguing
about what a good man should be.
Be one."

*Marcus Aurelius*

"I have a lifetime appointment and I intend to serve it. I expect to die at 110, shot by a jealous husband."

*Thurgood Marshall*


"Being a good husband is like being a good standup comic – you need ten years before you can even call yourself a beginner."

*Jerry Seinfeld*

"Work and children I could have.
But the husband was just
too much."

*Diane von Furstenberg*

"Always do sober what you said
you'd do drunk. That will teach
you to keep your mouth shut."

*Ernest Hemingway*

"When I read about the evils of
drinking, I gave up reading."

*Henry Youngman*


"The tragedy of machismo is that a
man is never quite man enough."

*Germaine Greer*

"Men should strive to think much
and know little."

*Democritus*

"Men have a better time than
women; for one thing, they marry
later; for another thing, they
die earlier."

*H.L. Mencken*

"You know… There is a name for people who are always wrong about everything all the time… Husband!"

*Bill Maher*

"A successful man is one who makes more money than his wife can spend. A successful woman is one who can find such a man."

*Lana Turner*

"Men can only be happy when they do not assume that the object of life is happiness."

*George Orwell*

"Why does a woman work ten years to change a man, then complain he's not the man she married?"

*Barbra Streisand*

"When a man steals your wife
there is no better revenge than
to let him keep her."

*Sacha Guitry*


"A man in love is incomplete until
he is married. Then he's finished."

*Zsa Zsa Gabor*

"In my house I'm the boss, my wife is just the decision-maker."

*Woody Allen*

"If it can't be fixed by duct tape or WD40, it's a female problem."

*Jason Love*

"Men wake up aroused in the morning. We can't help it. We just wake up and we want you. And the women are thinking, 'How can he want me the way I look in the morning?' It's because we can't see you. We have no blood anywhere near our optic nerve."

Sean Morey

"All women become like their mothers. That is their tragedy. No man does. That's his."

*Oscar Wilde*


"Every man needs two women: a quiet homemaker, and a thrilling nymph."

*Iris Murdoch*

"Anybody who believes that the way to a man's heart is through his stomach flunked geography."

*Robert Byrne*

"My mother-in-law's so fat that when she passes her handbag from hand to hand she throws it."

*Les Dawson*

"Behind every successful man is
a proud wife and a surprised
mother-in-law."

*Hubert H. Humphrey*


"Even money that my liver lasts
through my wife's metamorphosis
to my mother-in-law."

*Tim Heaton*

"I don't think my wife likes me very much, when I had a heart attack, she wrote for an ambulance."

*Frank Carson*

"Marriage: the most advanced form of warfare in the modern world."

*Malcolm Bradbury*

"Men tire themselves in
pursuit of rest."

*Laurence Sterne*

"My mom said the only reason men
are alive is for lawn care and
vehicle maintenance."

*Tim Allen*

"There is one thing I would break up over, and that is if she caught me with another woman. I won't stand for that."

*Steve Martin*

"Men are more easily governed through their vices than through their virtues."

*Napoleon Bonaparte*

"Men don't care what's on TV.
They only care what else is on TV."

*Jerry Seinfeld*


"The first rule of business is: do
other men for they would do you."

*Charles Dickens*

"A man's face is his autobiography.
A woman's face is her work
of fiction."

*Oscar Wilde*

"Men learn to love the woman they
are attracted to. Women learn to
become attracted to the man they
fall in love with."

*Woody Allen*

"One cannot be always laughing at a man without now and then stumbling on something witty."

*Jane Austen*

"A man's mother is his misfortune, but his wife is his fault."

*Walter Bagehot*

"People say nothing is impossible,
but I do nothing every day."

*A.A. Milne*

"Women cannot complain about
men anymore until they start
getting better taste in them."

*Bill Maher*